I0177406

Four Streams:
An inner-healing ministry

By David Colborn

Cover Design by Chris Edmonds

Copy Editor: Pam Minor

Four Streams: An inner-healing ministry

Copyright © 2013 by David Colborn

All rights reserved.

Published in Grand Rapids, Michigan by Heart & Life
Publishers, a division of Miles Media, LLC.
www.heartandlife.com.

ISBN 13: 978-0-9839924-9-3

Unless otherwise noted, Scripture quotations are from
The Holy Bible, New International Version®. Copyright
© 1973, 1978, 1984, 2011 by Biblica, Inc™. Used by
permission of Zondervan. All rights reserved worldwide.
www.zondervan.com.

Unless specifically noted by the author, names dates,
locations, and other details have been purposely changed
to protect the identities and privacy of those discussed in
the book.

To order more copies, please visit the author's website at
www.4theheart.org.

Printed in the United States of America

Contents

He sent forth his word and healed them . . .
Psalms 107:20

Introduction

We are living in a time that is blessed in many ways.
We have a medical profession that can increasingly do
wonders to intervene in our diseases and bring us back to
health.

I personally have experienced this. In my childhood I
had a heart condition that was periodically debilitating. I
couldn't play sports like other children. I didn't have the
energy to do many things. I was sick for long periods.

When I was fourteen, my doctor saw an article in a
medical journal about the first operation to correct my
condition. That year I underwent that operation and
received healing for my physical heart.

The results were dramatic. I suddenly had enormous
energy. Within months I was training for track and field
and within three years I was the top miler in my high
school. I had benefited from the direct intervention of
modern medicine. And God spoke to me just before the
operation and told me he was with me; that I would be fine.
I experienced both the intervention of medicine and care of
God via that intervention.

What I learned from my "heart healing" experience is that
God uses the good things man has discovered.

Throughout man's time on earth, God has provided inner
healing of the human soul. He has done this by divine
intervention and through deep experiences of his grace in
those who have sought him long and hard. He still does
this. It's part of his promises and part of his nature.

But God also takes advantage of man's learning and skills,
things that he has given us to bless us.

In our times, many of us are aware of diseases of the
human soul. We have learned that negative events in our

lives can have permanent effects. So we have developed psychology and counseling.

While reading *The Sacred Romance*, John Eldredge's first book written with Brent Curtis, I discovered that God cared about my non-physical heart. In the months that followed, I experienced my first taste of God's inner healing.

The insights I have received through reading the Eldredge books (*Wild at Heart* and *Waking the Dead*) and attending his men's retreats (ransomedheart.com), have shown me how to intervene in my own heart. I learned that God cares intensely about my heart and that he is only too willing to come and heal it. While John doesn't usually teach a step-by-step how-to, the process is there and I have learned from it.

The results have been amazing. I have new energy, passion and focus. Where I once was afraid of getting close with other men, now I seek out deep relationships with them. Where I found it hard to be a leader, I now relish leading groups to all the good things I've experienced. My relationship with my wife was once one of loving her for what she did for me; now it is one of just loving her for who she is.

As I continue to both receive inner healing and guide others to inner healing, I'm convinced that God loves this. I believe that he not only loves to heal those who seek him long and hard, but he loves to have us help in this process, to provide direct intervention just like my heart surgery.

My contention is that God loves to be invited into any form of healing, both of the physical body and of the soul. That's what I experienced as a boy and what I am experiencing now.

So now, in our culture and times, we are offered the

opportunity to invite God into the healing of our own hearts and the hearts of those around us.

But heart healing isn't the end. It is only the beginning. From a heart that suddenly has "capacity," comes the opportunity for identity from God. And from identity comes the opportunity for finding our place in the battle or our niche in God's plan for our lives. From a heart that is freed from much of the need to seek false comforts, comes the opportunity to walk with God. (For more on this, read all of John Eldredge's books.)

And a river went out of Eden, to water the garden; and from thence it was parted, and became four...streams.
Genesis 2:10 (Darby)

Chapter 1
About the Four Streams

This is a how-to book for people who want to learn the ways of guiding others to inner-healing. To do this we use prayer and invite God to come do the work. *The instructions are written using the male gender, but they are intended for women too.*

What are the Four Streams?

Four Streams is the use of four different avenues to bring life, wholeness and freedom to the heart. The Four Streams are counseling, healing and deliverance, in the context of discipleship. We use each of the streams as the Spirit directs. (Often this means using all four, but sometimes just one, two or three of them.)

The term Four Steams also is used as a general way of walking with God in community (see *Waking the Dead* by John Eldredge). Our use of the term here is focused on inner-healing. The other three streams of counseling, deliverance and discipleship are used to support the healing stream.

Why the healing stream is needed

The heart (inner or core self) has received a wound. This wound can be one large trauma or a series of smaller hurts that add up to a wound.

The heart, especially of a young child, is trying to figure out how the world works and this wound causes him to believe something about the world and himself that is usually a lie. For example, "I'll never matter."

The mind often comes to believe something entirely different, such as "With the right education, I can do anything." Or maybe, "With Christ I can do all things."

Until the heart receives healing there is conflict and tension between the heart and the mind. And the heart exerts the major influence over how a person deals with life.

As John Eldredge says in *Waking the Dead*, "We don't really develop our core convictions so much as they develop within us, when we are young. Certainly we'd reject the more disabling beliefs if we could; but they form when we are vulnerable, without our really knowing it, like a handprint in wet cement, and over time the cement hardens and there you have it. . . . what we've come to believe about those ultimate issues was handed to us early on, in most cases by our families."

So we develop our personal worldview, our model of who we are, how things work and how we should do things.

"On the basis of that model we:

- plan and make decisions

- interpret other people's actions

- make meaning out of life experiences

- solve problems

- pattern our relationships

- develop our careers

- establish priorities

"For each of us, our belief system is the filter through which we conduct the main task of our lives: making choices. It is no wonder that replacing the false parts of the belief system with truth can have such a significant impact on a person's life." *From Bob and Pat Reynolds' newsletter: The Good Report, Sept. 2003, out of Dallas, Texas, triadmin@ix.netcom.com)*

So, when we do Four Streams with someone, we ask Jesus to reveal the wound, the lie and any vow; we ask the person to renounce the lie and any vow; and we ask Jesus to bring a new truth that replaces the lie. When a person hears Jesus speak in his heart, he tends to believe and treasure it as the truth it is.

How I learned about Four Streams

I was introduced to Four Streams when John Eldredge demonstrated this method of inner healing in front of 60 men at a leadership retreat. The young man who volunteered was courageous. There were four sessions, about an hour each. I took notes as fast as I could. Something told me this was valuable and I needed to capture it. (See Chapter 8 for transcript of sessions called Four Streams Example)

On the last day we got to try Four Streams. We broke into six groups of ten and were told to find a volunteer and then lead him toward healing and identity, asking Jesus to come do the work. My group got a volunteer right away and some amount of heart work took place.

Trying it out

When I got home, I spent half a day with my wife asking her about her woundedness. I used Four Streams to guide her to freedom. She and I were thrilled with the results. We did Four Streams several times over the next months. I soon realized that learning how to listen to and guide my wife was a very good thing for our marriage.

I began to look for opportunities to guide men to freedom from wounds and their debilitating messages. Jesus came time after time and freedom resulted.

Soon I was serving as a Four Streams guide three or four evenings a week. The results were so gratifying and the closeness to Jesus so intense that I truly loved all of it—even the spiritual battles that proceeded, followed or occurred during the sessions.

Since then I have done Four Streams ministry with scores of people. The following is an attempt to share what I have learned with you.

Who can do Four Streams?

Four Streams is designed to be a peer-to-peer ministry. I am presenting it here, not for professionals, but for the common man. I think it is really good news that we can do this for one another. You can do this and there are a lot of people who need you to do this with them.

Another benefit of peer-to-peer ministry is that you can share your own heart, your own struggles with the person you are guiding. That is something that professional counselors are cautioned to avoid. We can be real.

All you need to remember is that you won't be doing this inner-healing ministry in your own power. You will be doing it dependent on God.

The purposes of a man's heart are deep waters, but a man of understanding draws them out.
Proverbs 20:5

Chapter 2
Preparing for Four Streams

To meet with someone and lead them into their deep heart, there are some prerequisites that you, as a guide, need to work towards.

- I cultivate a place of quiet and connection with Jesus in my heart. When I begin with a quiet, in-touch, heart, I can invite others to a place of rest. It is out of this place that a guide offers presence, safety and love. If my inner world is filled with distractions, I'm unable to offer the presence of the Lord and my own presence.

- Safety is important to guiding a person into the deep places of their soul. Not only should I offer confidentiality, but also the freedom to say anything without the fear of criticism or judgment. In this environment, the poser, or false self, can be left behind. The deepest secrets, fears, and shames can be shared safely. The one I'm guiding is accepted as he or she is because of the hope of who they may become.

- Love is a critical element of the relationship between the guide and the guided. Love provides safety from judgmentalism, impatience, and resentment. Love also keeps me from the temptation to make the person a project, to fix him. He wants to know I care about him. This is an area of weakness for me and I, myself need to go deeper with the Lord as I seek healing for others.

- Attentiveness causes me to focus on the other person and his experience. I have to set aside my tendency to analyze what he is saying or to plan how I will answer. This can be very difficult, but it is important to the man I am guiding.

- I must be willing to be touched by the feelings of the other person. I must be willing to cry along with him. The scripture tells us to weep with those who weep.

- I want to bring my heart connection with Jesus into the session. To do that, I need to keep my intimacy with Jesus fully alive. I need to meet Jesus regularly and sense his love and love him in return. I start with a heartfelt prayer for his presence.

- I must stand in my faith that Jesus will come and do his work in the one I'm guiding. The first time I did Four Streams, this was only based on the fact that Jesus came and healed my heart and spoke the words to set me free. After some experience as a Four Streams guide, my faith that Jesus will come was based on all those who have already received his love and healing. Bringing my confidence that Jesus wants and is able to heal, is a great gift.

- I need faith in my authority *in Christ* to deal with the enemy on behalf of the man. I want to be clear that my authority comes from Jesus.

- I stand in my dependency on Christ. Jesus must come or nothing transforming will happen.

Most of these preparation ideas are from the book Sacred Companions by David Benner, InterVarsity Press, pages 46-57. A wonderful book about spiritual friendship and direction.

How to get to the heart level

When I was first excited about helping people live from their hearts, I sometimes would walk up and ask one of my friends, "how's your heart?" The typical response was either confusion (what's he talking about?) or a wall (I can't get there right now).

There is an interesting hierarchy of conversational intimacy that helped me understand this problem.

Four levels of intimacy or communication

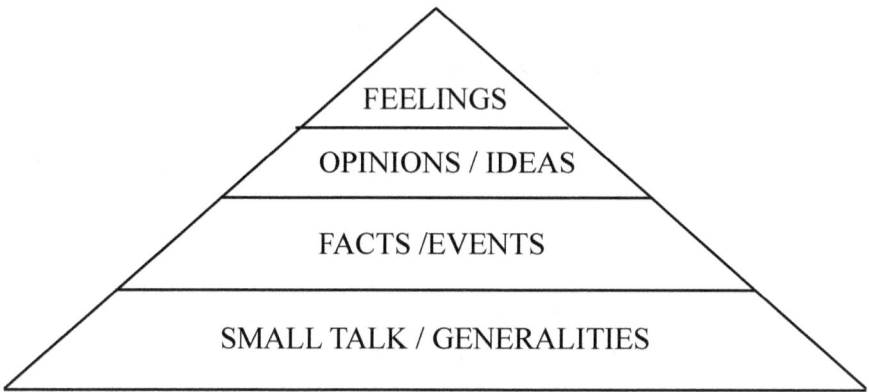

FEELINGS

OPINIONS / IDEAS

FACTS /EVENTS

SMALL TALK / GENERALITIES

Most people can handle intimate discussion better if we begin at the bottom and gradually work our way up to "feelings" and heart issues. By connecting through small talk and events in their lives, we can move through opinions and ideas and into the feeling level.

Getting to the feeling level is getting to the heart level which is where the real life is.

What the heart needs

Imagine that the heart is like the bed of a pickup truck. If it is full of pain caused by wounds, there is no way to receive God's love. Even though God's love is constantly available to be experienced, there is no room in the pickup bed. It is already full.

God's Love

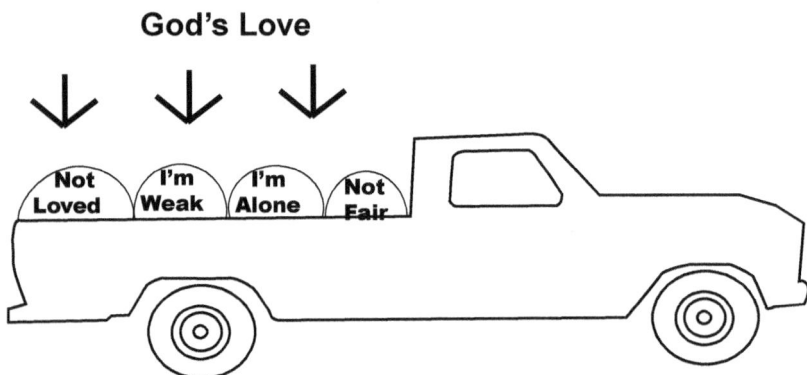

However, if God is allowed to enter the heart and bring healing, removing some of the pain, the heart begins to have capacity to receive love.

Imagine that God reaches in and removes the painful memories and messages. Little by little the bed is emptied and the messages are replaced by the truth.

I'm Loved | I'm Strong | Not Alone | God is good

Once the bed is emptied of lies and filled with truth, God's love continues to come and can begin to overflow to others.

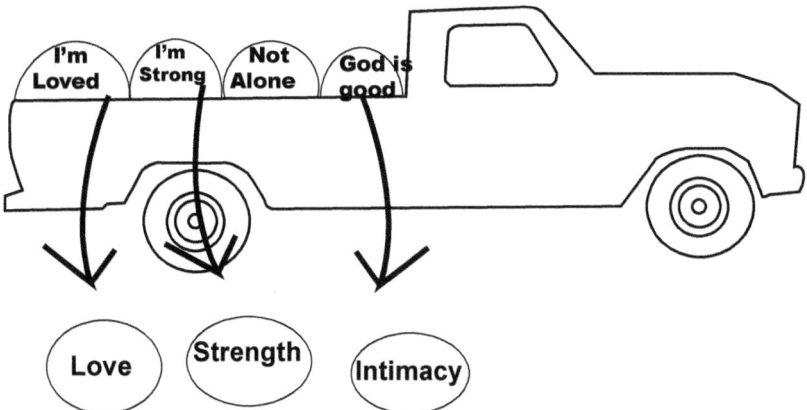

I'm Loved | I'm Strong | Not Alone | God is good

Love | Strength | Intimacy

He has sent me to bind up the broken-hearted, to proclaim freedom for the captives.
Isaiah 61:1b

Chapter 3
Doing Four Streams

In this chapter we'll start with the pattern that I use in my Four Streams work. The order is not sacred. There are many ways to accomplish the same thing.

Each element will be explained on the pages that follow under the heading Unpacking the Four Steams Pattern.

The Four Streams pattern I use

Getting acquainted

Often I begin by asking about his early life, especially their relationship with father and mother.

Opening prayer

Ask Jesus to surround us and for warring angels to protect us from the enemy.

"We give ourselves over to you, Jesus." (Get agreement from the person you're guiding.)

"We declare the authority of Jesus over our hearts." (Get agreement)

Discovery

"Jesus, reveal a wound you want to deal with." Ask him to report anything he hears, sees or senses.

"Jesus, will you grieve this wound with _____?"

"Jesus, show us the message he's/she's agreed with & any vows." Ask him to report anything he hears, sees or senses.

Deliverance

"Can you renounce the message and any vows?"

(If not, discover the name of the spirit that is oppressing and kick it out plus any backups. Then ask the question again.)

Countering the lie with truth

"Jesus, speak to him now and give him a message to

counter the lie."

When the truth comes, tell them to let the truth sink in on a heart level.

Forgiveness

"Can you forgive those who wounded you?"

"Can you ask God's forgiveness for sins that came as a result of the wound, the message and any vow?"

Counseling

Ask them to go back to the wound. "Does it feel calm and peaceful or is it still painful?"

If it is still painful, ask Jesus to reveal another message of that wound and so on until all is peaceful and calm.

Closing prayer

"Jesus unite the broken places of his/her heart. Make him whole, make him /her wholehearted."

"Jesus bring the young boy/girl into his/her grown up heart and unite them so he's/she's wholehearted."

"Holy Spirit/Jesus come and fill my brother/sister in all those new empty places." (Leave no room for the enemy's return.)

Praise, worship and thanks to the Father.

Counseling

Ask him to read Isaiah 61:1-4, with special emphasis on verse 4 where we, the healed ones, are to restore and rebuild. Ask him how the message and vow have affected their family and how the truth can now affect them.

End in prayer for the challenges, their spouse, kids, etc.

Tips

- Ask Jesus questions all through the session

- Command the enemy firmly—know your authority (see pg. 30)

- Avoid leaving wounds unhealed—the enemy smells wounds and returns 7-fold

- The enemy is a bully and goes after the young parts of us

- Encourage him to confess and disown the sins of the father, grandfather, etc.

- At the end, ask Jesus how to finish. Did we get it?

Unpacking the Four Streams pattern

Let's take each step of the Four Streams pattern above and expand on it.

How to get started

One way to begin doing Four Streams is to get a small group together in your home who want to learn with you. Simply focus on one person each time you meet. Go through the Four Streams process with that person and one person acting as guide. After each Four Streams session, leave some time for a "debrief" where you talk about what went well and what you would do differently next time. Soon you will be ready to offer Four Streams to others outside your group.

The environment

Pick a place where you will be undisturbed. Turn off all phones (yes, the mobile phones too). Plan for at least two hours of undisturbed time.

Remember what you are looking for

Before you begin, remind yourself of what you want to find, what you want to guide your friend to:

- Find an early wound. Early wounds (often 6 – 9 years old) have the most impact on a person's life. Later wounds are often related and build on this early wound.

- Find a message that comes from that wound

- Find any vows that resulted

- Look for logical connections between wounds, messages and vows.

Getting acquainted

I ask him to tell me something about his early life, with an emphasis on his relationship with his father, then his mother. I'm looking for possible wounds and messages, but I'm also establishing safety for him. I want him to relax and feel comfortable with me.

Opening prayer

There are three main elements here: Asking Jesus for protection so we can hear only from him; Giving ourselves to Jesus so he is the only spirit that can impact us; and giving him authority to enter every part of our hearts.

Notice that I address the prayer for both myself (the guide) and for the person I'm guiding. I think it is good to enter into the whole experience with the person you are guiding, rather than standing by the sidelines and coaching him.

My prayer is something like the following:

"Lord Jesus, come and surround us with your protective presence. Be here in power. And we ask you to send your warring angels to surround this property and keep any spirit of the enemy away."

(Get agreement from the one you're guiding on the next two prayer requests. Either have him say something like *"yes, Lord"* or repeat the prayer after you.)

"We give ourselves over to you, Jesus, completely. We say 'yes' to whatever you want. We dedicate this time to you and invite you to speak.

"We declare your authority, Jesus, over our hearts. We

open every hidden place in our hearts to you. We unlock
every door. You have complete access to us now."

Discovery—The wound

Here I ask Jesus to reveal a wound that he wants to deal
with. I'm hoping that we'll end up finding the childhood
root wound, but I let Jesus decide where we will go first.

So I ask Jesus to take us to the wound he wants us to go to
and I tell the man I'm guiding to report anything he hears,
sees or senses. Often people receive things from Jesus as
images instead of words; or sense things instead of seeing
or hearing.

What if the man has trouble hearing, seeing or sensing?

* You could ask him to tell you more about his young life
  and his relationship with his father (and mother). The
  father relationship is typically the most powerful. It is
  the father that most answers the questions of a boy's
  heart. (This is also true for a girl.) And it is the father
  that leaves the biggest wound. But sometimes a mother
  will leave a wound as well.

* If you know a man's place of strength and glory, expect
  a wound placed against that.

If we discover his wound or a man already knows his
wound, I start there. But later I ask Jesus if there is another
wound He wants to address.

> *Defining messages, lies, agreements and vows*
> Agreements are when we answer a suggestion such
> as "You're always blowing it!" with, "Yes, that's so
> true. I always do blow it. That's me." By making
> an agreement, we transform what might have been
> just a thought into an identity statement.
>
> When repeated woundings plant a message or lie
> that we hear over and over again, it can be easy to

27

give up and say, "Yep, that's true."

Often an agreement leads to a vow. Vows are strong statements of intention that may start with, "I'll never . . ." or "I'll always . . ." We are in effect digging our heals in and saying, "By God, this is how it will be in my life from now on!"

Vows have enormous power and Jesus specifically tells us not to make them (Matt. 5:33-37). He ends his command about not making vows by saying, "Anything beyond this [a simple 'yes, I will' or 'no, I won't'] is of the evil one."

Let me give you an example of a simple "no, I won't" versus what it would sound like as a vow: If the agreement is "I'm on my own," then a simple "no" might be, "I don't need John to come over to comfort me right now" whereas a vow might be "I'll never need anyone."

Vows give permission to foul spirits to join in their enforcement, making it harder to break an old pattern even if we want desperately to change.

Discovery—The message, lie & agreement

Every wound has a corresponding message or lie or agreement. These words are used interchangeably, even though "agreement" implies a strong acceptance of the message or lie. It is actually the message/agreement that hinders a person most. So finding the message/agreement is critical.

Start by asking Jesus to reveal the message that has come with the wound. Again ask the person you're guiding to report anything (really, anything!) he hears, sees or senses.

If the man is unable to hear, see or sense anything from Jesus, you can do a couple things:

- Ask Jesus if there is a spirit blocking his hearing. Often this is the spirit of confusion. Once you know the spirit's name, bind it and send it away.

- Or you can suggest a related message and ask the man if you are close. You can explore the possible messages together. Be sensitive to hear which one is most true in the man's heart.

Discovery—Vows
Often the man has made a vow related to the wound and message. It usually starts with the words "I will never . . ." or "I'll always . . ." Vows are very powerful and must be dealt with to get to freedom.

Ask him if he can renounce the vow. If he can't, check for a blocking spirit and dispatch it just as you did when he couldn't find a message.

A great example of a powerful vow is in the movie *Gone With The Wind* where Scarlet, totally impoverished by the war and responsible for several other family members, raises her fist to the sky and says "If I have to lie, steal, cheat or kill, as God is my witness, I'll never be hungry again." The rest of the story graphically illustrates the evil this vow causes for Scarlet, the man she marries for money, and many more souls.

Sometimes a man will have constructively dealt with a father wound, but will not have realized he is living under the influence of a vow.

Healing
Ask the man if he can invite Jesus into his heart to heal the wound. Another way to put it is to ask him if he can invite Jesus to accompany him into his wound. Ask him to let Jesus grieve the wound along with him. Tell him you'll both remain quiet for awhile and let the Lord do his work.

Sometime this goes easily, sometimes not.

If it doesn't go easily, probe to see what might be blocking his going to the wound or inviting Jesus to the wound. Sometimes it is just the intense sensitivity and pain of the wound that won't allow him to go there on a heart level. In that case, pray with him for courage and remind him of how critical it is to deal with this wound.

He may tell you he has no hope that this will do any good. Suspect a spirit of hopelessness and deal with it appropriately.

Deliverance—Direct deliverance

The most common tip-off that a spirit is oppressing a man is when he is unwilling or unable to renounce a lie or a vow, or unwilling to forgive someone. When this happens, I ask Jesus to show either of us the name of the spirit. Whatever names come to mind, I bind each spirit in the name of Jesus and send it to the cross of Christ for its judgment or tell it to "go where Jesus sends you." I have to believe in my authority in Christ (Eph 6:12).

If unable to hear the name of the oppressing spirit, ask what emotion he's feeling (check your own emotions too).

After dealing with a foul spirit, it is always amazing to discover that the man can then renounce a vow or forgive. (As soon as you sense the man you are guiding is gaining his strength, ask him if he wants to bind and dispatch the spirits you discover.)

Ask if there are more spirits involved and act on these.

Reluctance to forgive may have two other sources: sin or a misunderstanding of what forgiveness implies.

- If you sense that it is sin, ask the man if he is willing to ask forgiveness for his own sin of unforgiveness.

- He may have a misunderstanding of forgiveness.

Jack was abused by his father, and he initially was unwilling to forgive him. After some probing, it was discovered that, to Jack, forgiving meant that he might have to let his father abuse him again. When this misconception was cleared up, and Jack realized that he could forgive while not allowing any future abuse, he readily forgave his father.

Deliverance—Indirect deliverance

Some people believe in demons, but don't have a theology that allows for getting rid of demons directly (you telling the demon to leave in the name of Jesus). Or there may be a fear of dealing too directly with demons and stirring up the demonic world that then might attack the man with more intensity.

In any case, you can ask or sense what the man's tolerance for deliverance is before you start. If he shies away from direct confrontation of spirits, you could simply ask God to deal with the spirit. I'd say something like: *Father God, I ask you to bind and remove this spirit's influence on this man.*

An even more indirect approach would be to ask God to deal with the (human) spirit of _____ (unforgiveness, bitterness, discouragement, etc.). People are often said to have an unforgiving spirit, referring to their own spirit. Most anyone will be comfortable with a prayer that asks God to remove that person's unforgiving spirit (for example).

> *Deliverance surprise*
> John came for a healing session, but we never got to that. It soon became a deliverance session. He had been brought by his friend, Darrell, and Darrell wanted to be with us as we prayed with John.

I followed the usual path of asking for awareness of God's presence and asking him to send mighty, warring angels. Very soon John was unable to go forward, so I suspected some demonic oppression. Discerning what was in the way, we bound and sent away the spirit of unbelief. Then another spirit. Then another. Finally we had to sternly bind and dispatch the spirit of lust and were led to ask for John to have a spirit of respect toward women.

John began to experience some freedom. He told us he had a 10-year history of sexual encounters, that he was a sex addict.

I sensed the Spirit saying to have him break soul-ties with all the women he had slept with. After I guided him in doing that with two or three women, I asked him to lead in breaking ties with the next ones that came to mind. He did.

Then I sent him out to take a walk in the woods and continue to break the soul-ties (there were a lot of women on his mental list).

As John walked on a forest path breaking soul ties, he heard, "This is all BS. When you get home, you're going to go right back to this again. None of this is going to matter." John cried out, "God, I can't do this. You're going to have to do it."

John suddenly felt the presence of angels, one on his right and one on his left, walking with him. "I felt their presence, their largeness and I strongly felt their immense power. I started laughing. I realized that with their power, I could overcome it. All those past voices that said, 'You can't do this' stopped dead and in the presence of these mighty beings, I had faith that I could do the right thing with women in the future."

After John had left, Darrell told me with a shocked look that when I prayed for mighty, warring angels to surround us, he saw them arrive. He said they were about 10 feet tall and had big swords in their strong hands. I guess I believed that each time I prayed the prayer for angels, they did actually show up, but no one had ever verified that before. Wow. That increased my faith.

The other surprise from this Four Streams session was that John later told me he had been running from God for the last 10 years. In the years since this experience, he has been walking faithfully with Jesus.

Sometimes you begin expecting healing and end up going a totally different and critically important direction.

Countering the lie with truth
Asking for the truth
Having renounced the lie that he believed, now suggest he ask Jesus to speak into that memory a new message of truth. One prayer might be, *"Jesus, I invite you into that memory and ask you to tell me what you think of what went on, what you think of the lie I believed."*

Some other possible prayers:

- *"Father, what do you know about me?"*

- *"What's the truth about my heart?"*

Or

- *"What do you think of me?*

Sometimes a man will hear the truth in his head; often this is not helpful. If the truth he states sounds like it is from his head, ask him to stay in his young heart and try to hear truth there. He needs to experience Jesus speaking on a heart level, not a head level. And he needs the truth spoken to his young heart right where the wound happened. That's how the truth does the healing.

Another way of inviting Jesus to speak truth is by asking, *"Lord, where were you in this?"* Or *"Lord, how did you feel about this?"*

The Truth for Bobbi

In hearing Bobbi's story, it became clear that she was wounded early on by her parents' relationship with each other.

She told me about a typical time that she heard them arguing downstairs. She was drawn to come sit on the landing.

D: Bobbi, tell me about what life was like when you were young.

B: I felt insecure because my parents fought a lot. I would hear them downstairs in the living room arguing over something, and often I'd sit on the stairs so I could hear better, but not be seen. It scared me; what if they divorced? What would happen to me and my brother?

D: Why don't we ask Jesus into that. Let's let Jesus take you back to sitting on the stairs in your childhood home. . . Allow the memory to play like a movie. . . Let yourself feel what you felt then. . .

B: (Tears came) My parents are really going at it. I'm scared and feeling hopeless.

D: Stay with those feelings. . . What is the message or lie you hear?

B: That I won't have a good life; that relationships always turn out bad.

D: Let's ask Jesus, "Is there a vow?" Let me know

what you hear or see or sense from Jesus.

B: I don't think there is a vow. . .

D: Ask Jesus, "What is the truth to counter the lie of "I won't have a good life" and "relationships always turn out bad."

B: . . . I'm sitting on the landing, listening, and Jesus is sitting beside me, putting his arm around me. . . (tears) . . . He's saying to me, "I didn't want it like this for you. I wanted you to experience much more love between your parents." . . . Now I can see my parents still arguing, but they look weak and young. Jesus is sad for them; he wants to help them but they don't know he's here. Jesus stays with me.

D: How does that feel?

B: I feel bad for my parents, but I feel secure. I'm not alone. I'm important to Jesus. I'm going to be okay.

Counseling

The young boy

All of us have something young in us due to what life throws at us. Something in us gets frozen in time and often needs to be healed and integrated with our somewhat "mature" self. This is particularly true when there has been a deep enough wound to keep part of us back in grammar school, so to speak. It's like the boy has never graduated to become a man. He got stuck and is trapped. (See pages 84-85)

When you are dealing with a childhood wound, you are actually dealing with a young place, a memory that involves a child. I will often ask if the man had a nickname when he was a boy and I'll speak to the young boy by using that name.

So ask how the young boy is doing. How is the young boy feeling now? This will give you clues as to whether there

35

is something else going on that needs to be dealt with.

Young self versus mature self
Larry had read *Wild at Heart* and attended a
Ransomed Heart boot camp. He heard about me
from a friend. Since he was going to be in Dallas
for some training, he asked if he could come for a
Four Streams session. The session started with the
usual search for wounds, messages and vows.

We discovered that at about age six, his dad
had stopped reading stories to him at night. His
response was anger and the message was, "I'm not
loved anymore."

I asked Jesus to show Larry the truth about not
being loved anymore. Jesus revealed himself to
Larry's young heart in an amazing way: "I'm
experiencing Jesus jumping into bed with me,
tickling me and laughing."

I asked Larry to soak in the love, attention and fun
he was experiencing with Jesus.

Larry decided to ask Jesus, "Why did Dad stop?"

Jesus said to him, "Remember that your dad's
father died when he was two?" That explained a lot
to Larry's heart and made it easier to forgive his
father.

Larry told me, "I've treated my family the same
way I thought my father had treated me. He cut
me off, in my eyes." Larry wrote a prayer of
repentance in his journal: "Teach me to be present
to my family in love and not out of duty."

Larry found what sounded like a vow: "I have to be
on my own now." And as he pondered this, Larry
sensed a disconnect between his young self and

his mature self. His young self felt "agitation when something got rubbed."

We asked Jesus, "What is the place that gets rubbed?"

Larry heard, "Security . . . internal security."

Larry asked his young self, "Is there something I do now that makes you feel insecure?"

Larry heard, "When you get angry."

Larry decided to pray as a three-way conversation with his young self, his mature self and Jesus. He asked Jesus to help him get in touch with his young self and waited until he sensed this had happened. Then Larry asked Jesus and his young self for suggestions regarding dealing with his anger. Jesus seemed to say, "If you unite your young self and adult self, the anger will go away." Finally he asked Jesus, "What can I do to be united?" Larry sensed Jesus answer was, "Just allow me to do it for you."

We ended up the session reading the amazing scripture from Isaiah 44:21-23 (NLT). Here it is personalized:

"Pay attention, O Jacob [Larry], for you are my servant, O Israel [Larry]. I, the Lord, made you, and I will not forget you. I have swept away your sins like a cloud. I have scattered your offenses like the morning mist. Oh, return to me, for I have paid the price to set you free. Sing, O heavens, for the Lord has done this wondrous thing. Shout for joy, O depths of the earth! Break into song, O mountains and forests and every tree! For the Lord has redeemed Jacob [Larry] and is glorified in Israel [Larry]."

Is the memory calm and peaceful?
A wound can have multiple messages and it won't heal until all of them are countered by truth from Jesus. I learned this from Theophostic principles, another very similar inner-healing ministry. After finding the wound, the message (lie) and hearing Jesus' truth, there is a lot of freedom, even euphoria at times. But when things settle down, sometimes the wound hasn't really been dealt with. Going back to the wound, there is pain and discomfort.

I learned to return to a man's wound before the session was over and ask if it felt "calm and peaceful." If the wound wasn't healed, it was still a trigger to heart pain and the man would say something like "No, it still doesn't feel good there. It still hurts." I'd ask Jesus to show us another message associated with that wound. I'd keep after it until the memory was calm and peaceful. That seems to bring more consistent healing.

Prayer
Asking forgiveness
Consider suggesting that he ask forgiveness for mishandling the wound he has received; he may have had a choice as to how he reacted (depending on age). Potentially he could have taken it immediately to the Lord and avoided the debilitation a wound causes.

The young boy again
Here is where I ask Jesus to unite the young part of the man with the mature part of him. The idea is to help him become wholehearted. If the young boy is still separate from the mature part of the man's heart, there will be continuing conflict.

I pray something like: *"Jesus, come and unite the young boy with the mature man. Bring them together so they can communicate, so the mature part can counsel the young part. Make _____ wholehearted."*

If you sense that you are dealing with a driven adult (perfectionist, etc.), the uniting of the young and mature hearts may not feel safe for the young part. It probably won't happen at this time. Just be watchful for a later opportunity to bring these parts together.

Fill the empty places
Then I pray that the Holy Spirit will come and fill any empty places in the man. And I ask that the Holy Spirit seal all that has been done.

Praise and worship
Finally, I often suggest we have a time of thanks, praise and worship. We usually have much to be thankful for at this point. This usually takes the form of both of us praying. We might even sing a praise song.

Counseling
Ask him what questions he has about living this out. Or ask him how he thinks the new truth that he's heard from Jesus will affect his life.

Prepare him for the battle with the enemy. His enemy will try to re-establish the lie. He will need instruction on how to fight.

Have the man read Isaiah 61: 1-4. Point out to him that, having received healing and deliverance, he now needs to rebuild and restore as verse 4 points out.

Ask him how the lie he believed/embraced and the vow have affected his relationship with his family and others. Ask him how he expects the truth he has received from Jesus will affect these relations.

Final prayer
Lead him in prayer for the challenges he faces with his job, his friends, his wife and family. And, of course, anything else that comes up.

Set the next meeting

Always have your calendar available so you can set up another appointment to get together. Most men will need more than one session. Plan for several Four Streams sessions.

At some point you will sense that the healing work has been done. Think about continuing to meet, perhaps monthly, to help him deepen his relationship with Jesus. A good book to base your ongoing meetings on is *Sacred Companions* by David Benner.

He brought them out of darkness and the deepest gloom and broke away their chains.
Psalms 107:14

There is an old Hasidic tale that tells of a pupil who asks the rebbe, "Why does Torah tell us to 'place these words upon our hearts?" The rebbe answers, "It is because as we are, our hearts are closed, and we cannot place the holy words in our hearts. So we place them on top of our hearts. And there they stay until, one day, the heart breaks, and the words fall in."

Chapter 4
Going deeper

Tips

Here are some of the things I have learned about this kind
of prayer ministry.

I have to stay close to Jesus—keep my intimacy with
him. When I allowed ministry to guys to become the main
thing in my life, I got worn out and depressed. A friend
prayerfully offered this insight: "You're too focused on the
message and not enough on the Sender."

I am a Four Streams "guide." I'm not a minister, I'm not
a practitioner. I'm just a guide to help a man connect with
Jesus. I know "the way" since I've been there many times
for myself. (see also, Your legal position, below in Tips)

**A man shouldn't do Four Streams with a woman who is
not his wife**, because a lot of heart intimacy takes place in
Four Streams sessions. It isn't just about not being alone in
room with a woman not your wife. It's about the degree of
intimacy that takes place; the level of intimacy established
can lead to thought temptations and, ultimately, to sin.

My wife and I occasionally guide a woman together. This
seems to work out well with no lingering intimacy.

I ask Jesus to run things. Early on I tended to be more
directive: I'd listen to the guy's story and try to find his
main wound and then ask Jesus to come heal that. Later
I began to ask Jesus to take the man to the wound Jesus
wanted to heal. Most of the choices became Jesus', not
mine. I think it works better that way.

I can't know it all; I have to ask Jesus to show up. I
have to often remind myself that I can't figure out each
person's core wound, messages and vows. Often they are
well hidden. I have to invite our Lord to come and reveal

these things. This is the way it should be. God wants to be involved, especially in the healing of hearts. That is his specialty and he would be offended if we mostly left him out. And, we would be fools.

Not all guys are easy to help. Success after early success had made me feel like I could help anyone. Then I started doing Four Streams with guys who had deeper problems that didn't change overnight. A little humility entered my picture. When I asked Jesus about it, he affirmed me as a Four Streams guide and reminded me that I am a learner and always will be.

Time for each session: I usually plan for about 2 hours, but sometimes it takes 3. Occasionally it will happen in an hour, but rarely. Often the first hour is used in getting connected with the man, hearing his story. This is time well spent. Some men will require additional sessions.

I experienced what John calls "the man's warfare" in the hours before some sessions. I'd have unusual lustful thoughts or I'd be totally distracted and go from task to task never completing anything. When we'd get into our session I'd discover the guy was struggling with the spirit of lust or, in the other case, the spirit of distraction/confusion. When we'd bind and send those spirits away, there would be freedom to get healing and hear Jesus.

Like John taught us, our enemy tips us off without meaning to, and we can take advantage of this. Sometimes I'd be working with a guy and feel this emotion and hear in my head that this was going to be a big failure. Ah hah. We kicked out the spirit of discouragement that was oppressing the man, and he made progress.

Galatians 6:1 gives a glimpse of this: . . . *if someone is caught in a sin, you who are spiritual should restore him gently. But watch yourself or you may also be tempted.*

The healing isn't usually instant and permanent. My experience with wounds, including my own, is that they don't always go away completely with the first session. Yes, there is new freedom and release. But after awhile something comes up that triggers that same wound and it almost feels like you are back where you started.

This surprised me when it was my own wound. I thought I had that healed! I've learned to go back to Jesus with the new pain right away and ask for truth to replace the lie. I just do it as often as needed. Over time I feel like my own wounds are healing. They are less painful and I can go back there more and more easily when I need to.

Some men are healed on the first try, while others require years to be free of the wound and its message.

Prayer support is critical. The amount of prayer support needed for guiding a man to healing depends on the man's problems.

Men with difficult strongholds require more prayer support. Some inner-healing ministries recommend two to pray for the wounded man and two to pray for the guides (in those situations, they also recommend *two* guides).

The role of a Four Streams assistant. I have learned that it is very powerful to have a second person assisting in Four Streams sessions. Often this person is learning Four Streams and is not ready to function as a guide yet. His role is as an intercessor and a quality controller. Here are some tips for the assistant:

Continue protection prayers; pray for the receiver to push through to hearing from Jesus; avoid interrupting the flow from Discovery (finding the wound) through Countering the Lie (hearing the truth from Jesus); catch missed things; listen to the Spirit for additional things; listen to the Spirit for confirmation of what the receiver hears from God and share that with him; be sensitive to both the receiver and the guide. (Thanks, Merle Kroeker, for your input on this.)

Two guides can work together. If you ask another qualified guide to help in a session, decide as you begin which man should do what so you won't interfere with each other and confuse the man being guided. Recently I had my partner do most of the search for a wound and a message. Then I did most of the guiding when we got into the healing and deliverance.

Not everyone needs deliverance. About fifty percent of the men I have guided have appeared to need spirits sent away.

Soul ties are something you need to be aware of. These can be unhealthy, harmful emotional ties between people. For more on this, read the section called Soul Ties in Chapter 7.

Rhythm is usually established early on. You ask Jesus to reveal something. You ask the man to report what he hears, sees or senses. Soon he will report without needing your prompt.

Watch for distractions (new directions) at key intersections. Often a man will finish finding the lies he has believed and go to another subject. I interrupt and suggest that we ask Jesus for the truth.

Just spending time with a man, talking and praying over the deep things in his life, can sometimes bring deep healing. This happened with a man I met in California. As he talked to me (many words), I sensed that he had deep heart needs. I felt the Lord impressing me to say with strength and conviction "Jim, you are a good man." He immediately teared up. We met for a few hours the next day, sharing deeply. Later in the week I met with him again. He was a different guy. Something profound had happened. And I didn't do Four Streams with him, not at least in the prayer sense. Sometimes you are just not invited to do it that way, but you *can* share with another man what God has put in *you* and see a striking transformation.

Confidentiality is a critical part of your relationship with a man. Tell him that you'll be keeping personal things he shares with you confidential.

Your legal position is something you want to be clear on. You are a prayer guide. You are not a counselor (there are licenses for this) nor a minister (unless you are, of course). Present yourself properly.

Afterwards encourage him to journal the important elements of his Four Streams session. Explain to him that Satan will attempt to steal what God has said to his heart. By journaling and reflecting regularly on what happened, he will be strengthened greatly.

Sometimes a man will want to know more about something Jesus says to him. A great way to find out more about that is to just ask Jesus to explain. *"Tell me more about why you said that."* It is always amazing, but our Lord, the creator of the universe, loves to dialogue with us. He loves to answer our questions. He loves to keep the conversation going and our questions are a great way for him to accomplish that. I often ask a question and then more questions after that to get more into the details of what he is saying.

After your session you'll need protection. At a minimum, you'll want to bring the work of the cross between you and the man you've guided, between you and the man's warfare. If you have trouble sleeping that night, go through the bedtime prayer (download at TexasBandOfBrothers. org/resources)

What to expect

It might be helpful to give you an idea of the types of wounds, messages and vows that I have run into when doing Four Streams. This is not to say that you won't discover new ones. That is quite probable.

Notice that typical messages/lies all start with "I." They could just as easily start with "You." I believe these messages/lies are personalized

Typical childhood wounds:

- Father doesn't have time for me
- Parents withhold love
- Parents demand perfection
- Father won't connect with me
- Emotional separation from parents
- Father didn't protect me
- Physical or sexual abuse

Typical messages/lies:

- I don't have what it takes
- I'm not lovable; no one will ever love me
- I'll never get it right.
- I'm worthless
- I can never please him/her
- I'm on my own
- I'm shameful

Typical vows:

- I'll never try to do that again

- I'll never let anyone know that I need love

- I'll show them I have worth

- I'll never let anyone know my inner thoughts

- I'll never try to do something difficult

- I'll never need anyone else; I'll make it on my own

- I'll never trust anyone

Questions and answers

The men I've had the privilege of training to do Four Streams have asked some good questions which I think will be helpful to you.

Q. I understand that after healing a memory a guide should ask the guided to go back to the memory of the wound and see if it feels agitated and hurtful or calm and peaceful, and if it isn't calm and peaceful, to repeat the cycle looking for another message. But **what if calm and peace doesn't come to the memory even after three or four cycles** of prayer? What do you do then? Come back another day or another time? Or does this really seem not to happen?

A. You have the right idea: If the calm and peace doesn't come to the memory after a few cycles, then another appointment is called for. My experience, however, is that only a manageable number of messages are surfaced during a session. As life goes on for the man, he will run into that wound again and need to find additional messages and get truth and healing for them.

So it's the onion principle: You peel off as many layers as is practical, and then you come back to it as something comes up. I believe even the Ransomed Heart team is still having things "come up" in their interactions with one another.

Q. Also, **what if there is calm and peace after prayer, but the next morning they wake up and they are agitated and they feel like absolutely nothing has changed** (obviously many times this is a lie from the Enemy). But if you are not right there to help them with that, what do you tell them to do in that situation?

A. As guides, we need to prepare the guided for the battle that follows. Plus offering our phone numbers for triage and setting up another appointment for more instruction and perhaps more healing.

Q. **Asking forgiveness for mishandling a wound received as a young boy was something I wrestled with for a long time.** My line of thought was *"God, you allowed these wounds to come before I had perspective, understanding or reference in how to live life. How was I to know how to handle these wounds, I had not lived long enough to know!"* Yet, part of my healing process was to come to the realization that no matter what the age – we are responsible before God in how we respond to the events that come into our lives, even early on. What is your perspective on this?

A. You asked for my perspective on asking for forgiveness for mishandling an early wound. Here are some reasons that it makes sense:

I agree with you that there is a potential for handling the wound correctly, even at say seven years old: inviting Jesus into it for comfort, healing and truth. It might not be likely at that age, but it's possible. So it's good to get our mishandling of the wound off our conscience.

Mishandling the wound is also about the sins we have committed over our adult lives as a result of the lie we have believed or embraced. This is a heart thing, not a legal thing. We need to feel free of everything connected with the wound.

Instead of feeling a victim mentality, we need to take responsibility for what we have done.

Q. **How do we determine that a man does not need deliverance?**

A. I typically don't offer deliverance unless the man is blocked in some way (can't find the wound; can't find the message; can't hear God's truth; can't forgive; etc.).

Q. I realize that not all men are easy to help (no kidding), but **what do we do with the difficult ones?** A man has to want to be healed......... do we ever pass a man along or do we keep fighting and perhaps shortchange others who are willing?

A. We love them, for starts. We show them patience. We meet with them more than once, but not necessarily "forever." When nothing seems to work, we find out other resources for them and refer them.

Q. **Will Four Streams work for non-Christians?**

A. I believe it will. I know of a group in Indonesia who offer inner-healing to Muslims. When they get to the healing part, they check if it's OK to ask Isa (Jesus) to come and heal. Since Isa is in the Koran, there is no hesitancy. Once their heart has been touched deeply by Isa, they are open to knowing more about him.

Documenting your sessions

I almost always ask the person I'm guiding if he would mind me taking some notes during our session. I explain that it helps me keep track, and I'll be able to give him a copy of the things Jesus speaks to them.

Here are my reasons for documenting the sessions:

- Helps me keep track of the important elements in his story (often stories grow complex, even convoluted)

- Allows me to review for subsequent sessions, check progress, and discover things we haven't dealt with yet.

- I can send the person the words that we heard Jesus say so he can journal them.

Here's what I document:

- Name and date

- Main issues: father & mother relationships, wound(s), message(s), vow(s), truth from Jesus, besetting sins, struggles, and what Jesus has revealed in the past to him.

My eyes are always on the Lord, for rescues me from the traps of my enemies. Psalms 25:15 (NLT)

Chapter 5
Four Streams for yourself

Directions for guiding yourself to inner-healing

Here are some ideas on how to go to a wound for healing on your own:

- First, get alone so you won't be disturbed for an hour or so. Become quiet in your spirit and soul.

- Second, pray for protection by asking Jesus to surround you with his presence. Ask that you not be able to hear anything except from him; that the enemy's voice will be silenced.

- Third, ask Jesus to go with you. If you are not sure what wound, ask him to lead you to the particular wound he wishes to heal (if you are already feeling the wound, just ask him to take you into the memory of it).

- Stay with the memory and the pain of wound for a minute or two with Jesus there. Ask him to grieve it with you. Cry if you feel like it.

- Then ask Jesus to reveal the lie you believed as a result of the wound. Have your journal handy and write down the message (lie) of the wound.

- If there is a vow attached to the lie, renounce it out loud.

- Ask Jesus to tell you or show you the truth that will counter what you believed about yourself, God or life. When this comes, let the truth soak into your heart for awhile. And journal it as well. Very important stuff.

- Thank the Lord for his healing truth (the truth has a huge impact on healing the heart).

- Forgive anyone involved.

- Ask the Holy Spirit to close up any places that are open to the enemy.

- Maybe pray the daily prayer (download at TexasBandOfBrothers.org).

Prayers for guiding yourself to inner-healing

Here are a series of prayers designed for personal healing. They can be used by you, personally, or given to those who are ready to pursue healing on their own. They come from the Wild at Heart Field Manual by John Eldredge, pages 148 – 158, Thomas Nelson Publishers, Nashville.

- *Dear Jesus, I am yours. You have ransomed me with your own life. You have bought me with your own blood. Forgive me for all my years of independence. Forgive me for all my striving and all my retreating. Forgive me for all my self-centeredness and self-determination. I give myself back to you. I give all of me. I give my body to you as a living sacrifice. I give my soul to you as well. I give you my desperate search for life and love and validation. I give you my self-protecting. I give you all the parts in me I like and all those I don't. I give you my spirit also. Restore my spirit's union with you. Forgive me and cleanse me. Take me and make me utterly yours.*

- *Jesus, take me into my wound. I give you permission and access to my soul and to my deepest hurts. Come, and bring me to my own brokenness. Come and shepherd the orphaned boy within me. Let me be fully present to my wounded heart. Uncover my wound, and meet me there.*

- *Jesus, I renounce every vow. I made them to seal*

*off my wound and protect myself from further pain.
Reveal to me what those vows were. . . I break every
agreement I have made with lies that came with
my wounds. These are lies from Satan. I make all
agreement with you, Jesus. I give the protection of my
heart and soul back to you. I trust you with all that is
within me.*

- *Precious Jesus, I invite you into the wounded places of
my heart. I give you permission to enter every broken
place—every young and orphaned part of me. Come,
dear Lord, and meet me there. Bind up my heart as
you promised to do. Heal me and make my heart whole
and healthy. Release my heart from every form of
captivity and bondage. Restore and set free my heart,
my soul, my mind, and my strength. Help me to mourn,
and comfort me as I do. Grant my soul that noble
crown of strength instead of ashes. Anoint me with
the oil of gladness in every grieving part. Grant me
a garment of praise in place of a spirit of despair. O
come to me, Jesus, and surround me with your healing
presence. Restore me through union with you. . .*

- *Father, strengthen me with your true strength. Do it
by your Spirit in my innermost being. Let Jesus live
intimately in my heart. Let me be rooted and grounded
in love. I want to know the fullness of the love of Jesus
for me—its height and depth, its length and breadth.
Let me be filled with real knowing of your love—even
though I will never fully reason it or comprehend it—
so that I might be filled with all the life and power you
have for me. Do this in me, beyond all that I am able
to ask or imagine.*

- *Jesus, I choose to forgive my father for all the pain
and wounds he gave me. It was wrong and it hurt me*

deeply. I choose now to pardon him—because your sacrifice on the cross was enough to pay for these sins. I release my father to you. I also release any bitterness I've harbored toward him. I ask you to come and cleanse these wounds and heal them.

- *Father, who am I to you? You are my true Father—my Creator, my Redeemer, and my Sustainer. You know the man you had in mind when you made me. I ask you to speak to me—to tell me what you think of me as a man. I also ask you to tell me any name you have for me. By doing this, reveal my true strength— reveal what you specifically created me for. Open my eyes that I might see. Give me ears to hear your voice. Father, I ask that you speak these things not only once—but again and again so that I might really receive it. Now grant me the courage to receive what you say and the faith to believe it.*

In your childhood, if you'd been mature enough to ask Jesus to interpret a wounding event, you would have avoided the agreements. But now that you know how this works, you can do that whenever someone wounds your heart.

When the Lord brought back the captives to Zion, we were like men who dreamed. Our mouths were filled with laughter, our tongues with sounds of joy.
Psalms 126:1-2

Chapter 6
Four Streams stories

The stories that follow illustrate how Four Streams can be done in various situations. I have asked permission of the people involved to honor confidentiality and changed the names to protect their privacy.

Four Streams on the fly

We were staying with dear friends in their home and had just enjoyed Ron's walnut-banana pancakes (mmm). The kids had been fed and had disappeared to other rooms. We were just chatting and something from his childhood came up relating to his relationship with his dad.

I said, "That sounds like a wound."

Ron responded with, "Yeah, there were a lot of wounds from my father."

So I made a quick decision, I hoped was based on sensitivity to the Lord, and said, "And the message of those wounds was . . . ?"

Ron thought for only a second. "That I can never do it right."

Ron continued to share a bit and I heard something that made me suspect a vow.

"Could there be a vow that you made back then?"

"I think there was."

"And the vow was . . . "

Again, Ron was quite quick to answer. "I will never give my heart fully to any project."

Ron reflected on things he currently was doing and commented that he thought he was fully giving himself to them.

I asked him if he could renounce the vow. He said he could and did so. He went on for awhile praying to the Lord and asking forgiveness.

At this point I realized that we needed to hear from Jesus. We needed Ron's heart to hear the truth. As he came to a slight pause in his praying, I put my hand on his shoulder and said, "Ron, why don't you ask Jesus to come and speak the truth about your never doing it right, never good enough."

His chest heaved and I could tell he was hearing in his heart. I gave him a moment and then said, "Report to us what you hear."

"He's saying I am good enough. That he was happy with my work."

Ron was obviously moved by Jesus' words. I told him, "Let that sink in on your young heart level. Soak in what Jesus is saying to you."

Ron heard a few more affirming words. We asked God to seal up what he'd experienced.

Then Ron began saying that the areas he had thought he was fully giving himself to, he could now see that he was actually holding back. These were areas he cared intensely about: His relationship with his wife and kids and his work in medical school.

At that point we continued on with our conversation about life in general. This experience of Four Streams on the fly must have taken about 15 minutes.

Would you believe Four Streams via telephone?

I was asked by Henri if I could do Four Streams by phone. I had guided Henri in Four Streams at a boot camp, so we had that as a basis. A few months back, I had done Four

Streams on the phone with another man. Since Henri was living in Europe, and there was no way we could easily get together, I told him we should give it a try. We arranged a time by email and he telephoned me. Here are my notes from our session:

Rejection was the theme of Henri's wound. When Alleta hurt Henri, he would hide and wait for her to come restore things.

I asked why he didn't go to her and ask to talk about it. He said two things: He would feel dominated by Alleta, and she seemed to have more freedom (to be herself) than he did.

I asked, "When you think of going to her to talk about an issue, what feelings come up?" He answered: She's good and would listen, but she's not careful enough to not hurt me again.

I asked Jesus to show Henri an event, a wound, that relates to this.

"An event is coming to mind. I was about 14. My father was going through a bad time at work. He did something wrong (stole money) at work. In shame, he left home (for a few hours), leaving a letter that told about what he did and how he felt. After mom read it, I read it too. We didn't know he was coming back."

I asked Jesus to show Henri what message/lie he got from this event.

"I'm on my own. I should take care of myself."

I asked the Lord to come and speak the truth regarding the event.

(Jesus speaking) "I was there. I saw the pain that everyone had. I was hurting myself. I was sustaining everybody. I didn't leave your father alone. I didn't forsake him. He had to go through that. He had to feel the pain. I had some deep dreams for your whole family."

(Henri speaking) "My father subsequently tried to kill himself with large doses of medicine. He was unstable for 1-2 years. It was devastating to see my father wanting to kill himself."

I asked the Lord to tell Henri what the message/lie was related to the suicide attempt.

"Father cannot help me with tough situations. I have to do it myself. When things get very tough, maybe it is better to leave this world. I won't be strong enough; I'll be just like my father."

I asked for the truth:

"I am your strength. I made you, live in you. I am your spinal cord (backbone). Together we stand. I want to be strong with you. I want to fight with you, together in the battle like two brothers in arms."

Henri: *"Forgive me for not believing I can be strong. I refuse to hide in meekness and failure. Forgive me for concealing my strength by hiding. I confess I didn't believe that you could be strong in me and we could be strong together. I was afraid of your big dreams. Forgive me for this time wasted. I bring all this at your feet, at your cross. I accept now what you want to do with me. I want you to grow in me now.*

"I want to fight your battles, follow you, be your brother. Please let me always be behind you, behind your shield."

Is there a vow?

"Sort of. There is no escape from the same fate my father experienced."

Henri declared this untrue and said: "I'm different from

my father. I'm the Lord's. I have nothing to fear because my days are in the hands of the Lord."

"Lord, can I have a vision like the previous times we've done Four Streams?"

"Previously I saw I was like King Arthur on my horse with the armor of the Lord. I was set apart for God to conquer. It makes my heart jump."

"Now I see a new version of this: The Lord is also with me and we're riding together, teasing each other to see who will be the fastest. First we're standing still and discussing and then we're racing."

I asked Henri what he thought that meant.

"It means I'm to take back the territory from the enemy. For myself, my family and my friends."

My experience of doing Four Streams over the telephone has been good, but not as good as being there with the man. It takes much more sensitivity since there are no visual clues. You are relying on what you hear and sense spiritually. I would only do it when there is no other practical means to get together and there is a strong need.

Steve gets a gift from Jesus

Steve's mother never let him play with guns or swords or anything war-like.

When Steve heard the truth from Jesus in his young heart, I took him a step farther. "Steve, why don't you give the lie you've believed to Jesus?" I paused to wait for this and he told Jesus that he was giving him the lie he'd believed for so long.

Then I said, "Steve, look and see if Jesus has a gift for you."

With tears streaming down his face, Steve said, "Jesus has

given me a sword. (Pause) But now he's encouraging me to play swords with him. (Pause) We're having fun together!"

It is truly wonderful to have Jesus meet us where we are and give us what we deeply need.

Confusing beginning

Keith, a full-time missionary, told me he was angry with God for not answering his prayers for many years. He said he felt ashamed he was such an infant spiritually. The following is Keith's dialog with God about this.

K: *What do you want me to do about that?*
God: I want you to grow in the disciplines.
K: I feel such hopelessness. (We prayed about this and bound and sent the spirit of hopelessness away. Then I suggested Keith ask Jesus for hope.)
K: I don't feel any change in my hopelessness.
David: What have you experienced about God's presence?
K: I feel like a little mouse before a monumental God on a throne. My squeaking is so insignificant . . . I'm feeling seething anger. Lord help me through this anger. I want to be freed of this anger so I can receive your love. Soften my heart. . . Now I'm getting a picture of how often I get frustrated with my daughter and say, "Why don't you trust me to do good and give you good things?" I'm stuck, just like my young daughter.
We continued to sit with Jesus.
K: My life has just flashed before my eyes; all the good things that have happened, all the blessings. There has been so much good, so many blessings. . . Thank you Jesus. Help me to be thankful for all you've done. I ask forgiveness for my ingratitude, my pride, my selfishness. . . I'm experiencing peace . . . I feel like my heart is softening. I sense his invitation to spend a lot more time in his presence and to bring whatever emotion I have at the time. He's saying that then good things will happen: growth, fun and blessing.

K: Now I'm seeing a picture of me with Jesus. He's at a desk, hard at work. I'm there with him at peace. He knows I'm with him. I'm not demanding my way. It's okay that he's doing what he needs to be doing. We're connecting anyway.

Four Streams in married life

On June 9th, 2004, I asked my wife, Barbara, the Big Question, "How am I wounding you?"

D: How am I wounding you? . .

B: When you cut me off because you think you know what I'm going to say or when I take too long to say something.

D: What is the message to your heart when I do those things?

B: "I'm not important to you. You'd rather be with the guys than with me."

D: Wow. Anything else?

B: I wish you would support my dreams for a beautiful yard. When I ask you about it, you get conservative about spending money and energy on it.

D: What message do you get from this?

B: "You're not that important. Your dreams aren't that important."

D: I see.

B: I hate to give you a "honey do" list, so I go too far in the opposite direction—I don't ask for what I want. If you don't help around the house, I think, "He doesn't care about that. It isn't important to him."

D: Hmm. There's probably a message there as well.

B: The message is, "Our home isn't as important to him as his activities." And "He'd rather be with the guys than with me."

D: Lots to look at for me.

Postscript from David: It helped me a great deal to hear all of the ways I was wounding Barbara. I want to believe I've wounded her less in those ways in the years that have past.

But it took eight years before I caught the "beautify the yards" bug—and that had to do with the healing of my own heart. In the year before writing this account, I let go of a number of activities that had been more about my own need to be accepted by other men than they were about ministry. That left me with energy to put into Barbara's dream. Once I dug in, I found landscaping deeply satisfying and a challenging adventure. And some of the guys even came over to help me.

Caveat: I don't recommend you ask "How have I wounded you?" unless you're willing to hear the truth without being defensive—otherwise you risk adding to the wounding rather than being used to bring healing! Start with less potent questions like, "What makes you come alive?" and later try, "What was your father like when you were growing up?" before asking the BIG QUESTION.

Brother wound

Harris was burned out on spiritual disiplines. He sensed he was stuffing his emotional needs in order to give more to ministry. He received counseling earlier that revealed the need to find out who Harris is and to start asking for what he needed.

He also had been feeling lonely at home.

When we met one evening, we really didn't have an agenda, but it turned into a healing session. Here's how it went:

It became obvious that he didn't allow himself to have desires and wants.

D: Lord, what memory is associated with not having

desires and wants?

H: My brother came to mind.

D: Why, Lord?

H: I feel like I have to walk on eggshells when hes' around.

D: And why is that, Lord?

H: I try not to rock the boat.

D: What about his brother causes this, Lord?

H: He's over-emotional. I feel like I'm trying to live up to him. Not so much my dad, because I didn't grow up with dad.

H: I wanted to please my brother so he'd like to be around me, I wanted to be worth something in his eyes.

H: He talked down to me a lot. Made me feel inferior physically, mentally and in giftedness.

D: Lord, what was the message Harris received from all this?

H: I'm not worth it. I don't have the same worth, I'm not as valuable.

D: Was there a vow?

H: I'll never be like him. I'll always be inferior.

D: Can you renounce those vows?

H: I think I can.

He renounced the vows and immediately said, "I have just as much worth as my older brother."

D: Let's ask Jesus to bring his truth to that.

H: I'm reliving a memory with my brother and Jesus is there too. He's put his arms around me and is saying, "You have worth, Harris. You are my beloved son."

H: I'm having another memory. I'm in middle school listening to my brother talk. I said something that upset him and I see myself squirming my way back, feeling diminished.

H: But Jesus is there too and he put his hand on my shoulder to reassure me.

Though my father and mother forsake me, the Lord will receive me.
Psalms 27:10

Chapter 7
Special situations

When I began guiding men to healing and freedom, I
knew relatively little about the human heart. The desire
was there to help; the passion for their freedom; and the
rudimentary pattern of how. But as my experience grew,
so did my understanding. So will yours.

What follows are some ideas for dealing with special
situations. You won't need them for every guy, but after
you've had some experiences, you'll probably run into one
of these situations. So here's a heads-up.

Unforgiveness

Ed had a real problem. His wife had had an affair, waffled
for awhile between Ed and the other man, and then
divorced Ed, took their young son and married the other
man.

Ed had been able to forgive his wife, but not the man. He
realized that he'd tried to forgive the man repeatedly, but
later ended up furious with him and would have to start
the forgiveness process over again.

I led Ed through a powerful way of forgiving. It is based
on a banking analogy. At the end of the year, the bank
looks at its list of debts and decides which ones are
uncollectible. The bank then takes its own, good money
and uses it to write off each uncollectable debt. The debt
then is paid. The bank no longer seeks payment. In fact,
if the debtor were to show up with money to pay the debt,
the bank would refuse saying, "That account is closed.
You no longer owe anything."

Bank	Writes off bad loans	Balance Sheet
	• Loan xxx • Loan zzz • Loan yyy	Assets Loans $xxx Property $zzz Liabilities xxx $yyy xxx $zzz Net Worth $xxx

So I asked Ed if he could take from some of his own good will and move it over to this man's debt account (the emotional debt this man still owed him). I made it clear that once he did this he could no longer see this man as owing him anything. The debt would be paid. The account closed.

Ed and others have done this. Afterwards they have remarked that it was a very powerful experience and a forgiveness that lasted. The power in this is that the forgiver has actually "done" something. Later, when they would think of the person who had wronged them, they would remember that they had paid for the debt themselves.

Soul ties

Soul ties are just what they sound like: ties between the souls or hearts of two people.

There are healthy and unhealthy soul ties.

Healthy soul ties are illustrated by the relationships of David and Jonathan and Naomi and Ruth. Obviously husbands and wives are meant to experience healthy soul ties.

Unhealthy soul tie examples include relationships characterized by manipulation, guilt, emotional abuse, co-dependency, unnatural affection, envy and/or lust.

Sometimes the relationship between a mother and her son or daughter is an unhealthy soul tie. These relationships may be characterized by manipulation and guilt, perhaps co-dependency.

How to know if you have a bad soul tie:

Ask the Lord: Take a moment to ask God in prayer to show you any unhealthy soul ties.If the Lord brings people to mind or you think there is a possibility of an unhealthy soul tie, proceed to pray to cut the soul tie.

Look at the fruit: A way to determine the nature of a soul tie is to examine its fruit (Matthew 7:16-18). Good soul ties will bear good fruit; examples being love, blessing, fidelity, loyalty, honor, righteousness, etc. The overall effect of the good soul tie will be to strengthen our emotional wholeness and our walk with God. Bad soul ties will bear bad fruit, examples being hatred, resentment, curses, manipulation, anger, strife, jealousy, control, bitterness, envy and lust.The overall effect of bad soul ties will be to hold us back from enjoying our relationship with God and to keep us in bondage to whatever we struggle with.

Cutting soul ties: We can cut soul ties by praying in the authority of Jesus Christ. The idea is to cut the ties in Jesus' name and ask for restoration to wholeness. Here's a sample prayer:

"In the name of Jesus Christ and by the power of his blood shed on the cross, I cut myself free from any unhealthy soul ties that may have been established with _____ (name), Please restore me to wholeness in spirit, soul and body and reintegrate any part of me that was involved with those soul ties. I commit him/her to your care to do with as you will.Thank you, Lord, for your healing power and your perfect love for me. In Jesus' name, Amen."

Based on excerpts from the website, freeinchrist.truepath. com

Generational curses

Sometimes it will become apparent that there may be generational curses involved. This means that parents, grandparents and so on have been involved in the type of sins that this man is struggling with. The effect of these sins has been passed down to him and, if not challenged, will be passed to his offspring (Exodus 34:7)

After explaining generational curses and their results, you can ask the man if he will renounce and break the generational curses. Have him name the particular sins that he and his ancestors have committed. Have him repent for himself and his ancestors. Finally, have him break the curses that have resulted from these sins repeated generation after generation. Here's a sample prayer:

"Because of Jesus' blood, I ask forgiveness for the sins of my ancestors and of myself. Specifically, the sins of _____. I renounce these sins and ask your mercy and grace to be done with them. I break the generational curses that have been passed down. It ends with me. In Jesus' name, amen."

Disassociative Identity Disorder (DID)

When a child experiences a severe trauma, God has arranged for relief from that horror. The child will often box off that experience and won't be able to remember or feel associated emotions.

This disorder is much more complex than we are prepared to deal with using Four Streams. The best thing to do is to refer a man that you suspect has DID to a qualified practitioner.

The tip-offs are mainly two:

1. Inability to remember and/or have emotions about large portions of his childhood.

2. His telling you about traumas (someone else has told him about) that you suspect would cause disassociation.

For he breaks down gates of bronze and cuts through bars of iron.
Psalms 107:16

Chapter 8
Four Streams example
(John Eldredge and Lon)

At the Ransomed Heart's first Advanced boot camp, John devoted an hour each day with a young man doing Four Streams. This was in front of 60 attendees.

At one point he asked the men he works with at Ransomed Heart to come up and assist. They were Craig, Bart and Gary.

John is a skilled counselor and, in this example, models how to use Four Streams for inner-healing.

Lon's name was changed to protect his privacy; he has given his permission to share these sessions.

Session 1

J. I know very little about Lon's story. The willingness to jump into the unknown is essential to masculinity and walking with God.

J. prayed:

1. For eyes to see and ears to hear.

2. For light. Surround us with light.

3. Asked Jesus to take us right to the issue.

I want to be brought up to date with current issues and then early issues.

L. After boot camp I was restless inside. A friend asked about my struggle with pornography. He said it was adultery against my wife. I told my wife this and she requested that I get counseling. From then till now has been recovery. I got counseling from December to August. But I wasn't able to stay sober. I thought I'd pay the money for the counseling and ask God to take it away. The counselor said if it keeps up, he'd have to counsel Jean as well. He said my words to her were "stay," but my actions were "go." Something happened that has caused me to stay sober.

J. How are things with Jean?

L. She's beginning to trust me. She's starting to deal with her own heart. She has a tendency to emotional absence. I'm starting to use your message with her.

J. Tell me about your past, your background.

L. I spent time with my dad and his brother (Uncle Steve). Dad taught me to hunt and fish, but Mom did the discipline. When Mom was gone, he didn't discipline me.

J. Your relationship with your dad over the years, what was it like?

L. Sportsmanship came before competition. He was big on academics, then college, then a good job.

J. Was there delight in you from Dad?

L. He had his own life. I felt like I was on his stage. Part of it at times.

J. If you did what?

L. Did well in academics and sports, then I was included for a time.

J. It struck me that you said that with so little emotion: "I could be on his stage if I performed."
L. My family life seemed okay compared to others.

J. What about the counseling you've received has struck most core to you?

L. Not sure. It explains me. It is important to linger in it.

J. Which leaves you feeling what?

L. That life is difficult. Not much direction.

J. You told me Mom did the discipline. What was your relationship like?

L. She was structured, but affectionate. When my two-years-older sister left for college, she started serving me more. When I left for college, I built my relationship with Christ. She was my best friend and mentor and we were sounding boards, for each other.

J. How would you characterize how you could please her?

L. Behavior.

J. The things that you have just accepted are tragic and heart breaking. A boy needs mercy, love and kindness from his mom. From dad he wants "delight in me." You had none of either. It gets to me that you accept it. The dismissal of it. That acceptance of it is a big part of why your heart is pinned down. "Other boys have it worse." Somewhere in that your heart shut down. Can I ask you what you're feeling right now?

L. I'm feeling like I don't really want to go there. I'm holding back. I've been down this road so many times; it seems futile. (tears)

J. Beneath the tears is a desire for . . .?

L. I don't have words to express . . .

J. If you were really able to walk through this, how would you feel?

L. That's why I'm here.

J. See the desire is still there. It has been buried and disappointed, but it's still there. The fear of going there is . . .?

L. I'll be disappointed one more time.

J. If your life could be what you wanted it to be, what would it look like? With Jean? With God? With yourself?

L. I don't know. The progress helps. I have desires for ministry, but it's not for now. I'd like more connection with Jean and my friends.

J. You use the phrase "I don't know" and that is in the way. It is a protective mechanism and agreement with the enemy. Then you don't have to go there and be hurt again. If you want freedom and connection with Jean, you're going to need to know. Look it square in the face. Do you see that?

L. Yes.

J. What does that cause you to feel?

L. Fear and hope.

J. You realize that your pornography addiction has nothing to do with sex?

L. It's self entitlement. My right to feel a high. It's a feeling of connection versus isolation.

J. You realize you don't have any connection with anyone else except your uncle?

L. That's why I'm here. I want to only be with people I trust and don't have to put up a façade. I was tempted to try to springboard off your life. Jean said go, so I'm here.

J. That brings tears. Why?

L. I don't know. I feel like I don't deserve it. . . . I want life, the real thing.

J. Lofty ideas bring tears?

L. I don't know.

J. Would you be willing to let Christ take you there and

help you to know?

L. Yes.

J. I'll pray a simple prayer and you repeat it, OK?

L. Yes.

J. Jesus take me to the true issues of my life. Walk with me there. Any covenant or agreement I've given to denial, I cancel.

Where did you go?

L. Trying to think . . .

J. You don't have to analyze our analyzing. Just stay present with me and current and we'll get there.

L. I felt loved . . . (crying)

J. Tears are good. Grief over being loved. Your tears help that. You should journal about your grief at being loved. You have fears about being alone. What's the smile?

L. A feeling of being rescued.

J. What if Jesus had just come for you alone?

We'll get this. There's more, but I'm with you. My suggestion is you just go journal and we'll connect at lunch. (L. left the room.)

John to all of us: What rises up in you? Don't analyze.

Group: The need to rescue. Empathy.

J. The intense desire to set him free. That's what it takes. Men don't want to be a project.

Session 2
Warrior type prayer

J. I'm curious how the afternoon was.

L. The lie actually matters. It makes a difference that I believed a lie.

J. That was good. Well handled. You said there was no place to hide. Hide what?

L. Hide my sin. Hide in my false self.

J. Yeah (3x). And hide anything else? What felt most exposing in our time?

L. I'm a burden. I'm taking up their time. This is not a good use of their time. If I can't join in, I'm a parasite.

J. Was that what pharmacy school was about? Was being a pharmacist your dream?

L. I didn't have a desire for anything, from when I was young.

J. No place for dreams?

L. I enjoy what I'm doing right now.

J. Here's a wild thought: What if you were meant to connect with people?

L. That's part of what I do.

J. But the level of deep connection is nil. The message from your parents was "Let's not connect. Go to work." The permission to desire connection needs to be happening. There needs to be permission to be needy.

L. I don't know how to keep from letting that go too far.

J. We're really talking about the boy who really wants to be known. Who is dismissed, disciplined, told to work. I don't care about your grades, your work. I want to know you. What do you want to do?

L. Go fishing, stay up late and talk. Break a few rules.

84

J. What do you let your boy do?

L. When the work's done, have some fun.

J. Sounds like he's locked up in a box. In many ways you're treating him like your parents treated you. You're acting in the role of parole officer, counselor, pastor. You don't have to do that. There's got to be some part of you that is really weary of that.

If I really saw you, what are you afraid I would see?

L. The fears I have. That I'll be caught off guard.

J. If you were caught off guard, what would I see?

L. Panic.

J. What's beneath panic and fear? That if I saw the real you . . .

L. I'm not interesting.

J. The boy wants out. What's keeping the boy from coming out is the fear that you'll be uninteresting. That's worse than people knowing about your addiction.

I'm going to shift gears and pray. I'm going to bring in a couple of streams. (Healing and battle)

I want you to realize that you don't have to work at this to get it. The enemy has taken your desire for connection and turned it into shame.

I'm pissed, not at you, but at what the enemy has done.

Speaking to group: You'll spin your wheels when there is something blocking. That's why I turned to prayer.

J. Jesus what is going on here?

Answer. A shroud is over him.

J. What is the shroud?

Answer. Shame and guilt.

J. Lon, what are you feeling right now?

L. Indifference.

J. The source of that is Mom and Dad.

L. It shifted to "Getting free doesn't matter."

John called in his band of brothers to join the warfare:

Craig said later, that as he approached he himself felt overwhelmed by deep resignation and hopelessness. Then he thought, wait, this isn't me. Maybe I'm feeling what's going on in him. (Spiritual warfare works like a computer virus: it tries to jump from one person to others.)

Gary felt "I don't matter. If I mattered, God would fix it."

Bart had a sense of worthlessness. The accusation was "you've lived with this a long time, you can live with it still. It's not such a big deal.

J. I asked Jesus what to do first.

Answer: There's a shroud.

J. In the authority of Jesus I bind and remove this shroud. (Then fought the spirit of indifference.)

(Often, when you are going to help someone, their warfare will come against you ahead of time.)

Next, John led Lon in prayer so he would exercise his will. "I take everything suicidal under the atonement. I break all agreements with indifference."

Finally, John asked Jesus what he needs (don't leave his house empty).

- Affirmation

- You matter

- We'll fight for you

(Gary waits for freedom to lay hands on someone. This helps avoid transference of spirits.)

The kingdom is based on authority, so agreement with the enemy's lie gives the authority to the enemy.

Session 3

J. How are you doing now?

L. I didn't think it would be this hard. I had a good time of prayer with Tim. I realize I'm not being a burden. On my way to my room I felt like Private Ryan.

J. You're worth fighting for. Where's your level of hope today?

L. Lot more hope today. I don't want to just manage; don't want to just fit in.

J. This invitation, I want you to know, is to all of you. I want to enjoy what I find there. Nothing in me expects to be disappointed.

What about warfare makes sense?

L. The indifference, shame and guilt. I see I've made agreements.

J. Is there any opposition?

L. Not since yesterday afternoon. I need some help with when to express my feelings; I know they are not all good.

J. Something in you wanted to help others, to move out of the technical. Have your parents supported that idea?

L. With attachments.

J. Your heart has been under a long assault to shut you down. To shut down connection. That is the very thing you are strong in. The intentional war is to keep you from using connection.

L. There's been a narrow window of opportunity to do connection. It's been restricted.

J. You have to make a heart very small to fit into those restrictions. With us, I want you to come out and be a burden. I want to pray for unhealed areas, to peel that stuff off so your heart can come up for air. We'll ask Jesus what's here that we need to deal with. (At this point I felt the subtle message "So John, you are not up to counseling him out of it yourself? You need others?")

Lon, I'll trash the entire weekend to get you free.

There seems to be a sense of self-hatred: one part won't forgive another part. Addictions?

L. Yeah. I feel resentment toward the part that desires unorthodox freedom and adventure. I just wish I'd be content.

J. Jesus, where did that begin? Where did the "I want too much," start? Did it come from Mom?

L. When I was with others and having a good time, she would shut it down. "It's time to stop." Having fun and letting go would get me in trouble like scolding and discipline.

J. What would be your Mom's words?

L. I don't remember.

J. We're going to pray. The boy wants to come out and he needs forgiveness and permission. It's time to offer forgiveness to him for getting you in trouble, for getting scorn and shame. Release of resentment will help us get this stuff off.

(John led Lon in prayer, having him repeat.) Forgive me Jesus for any sinfulness in all this.

In the authority of Jesus, we come against the spirits of self-reproach and resentment. We bind you from him. We send you to the feet of Jesus for your judgement. All underlings included.

Jesus, what else is set against Lon?

- Doubt
- Confusion
- Need to forgive parents
- Shame

Lon, report any messages or thoughts to us as we go along.

Repeat after me: "Jesus, forgive me for relying on my mind."

Lust is a servant of shame. Shame happened as a little boy. Lust came along later to keep the shame alive. That's not you; you have a good heart.

In the authority of Jesus, I bind the spirit of lust and shame . . .

There is a soul bond. We should only have a bond to Christ.

Repeat after me, Lon. "Jesus, come and break all soul ties between me and my mom."

In the authority of Jesus, every spirit that is not of Christ be bound and leave.

Angels of Christ, take them out of here immediately or, if they won't go, destroy them immediately.

Repeat after me, Lon. "I invite you, Jesus, into the abandoned places. I forgive Mom. I release her to you Jesus. I forgive Dad and release him to you."

I want to speak to that young boy in your heart. You may hear from him (the young boy). If you do, share what you hear.

(Speaking to the young boy.) We love you. You're safe. We want to meet you.

J. Lon, what are you feeling right now? (in a soft voice through this segment)

L. I don't know if I want to be known.

J. How old are you?

L. Five.

J. Why don't you want to be known?

L. I'm frightened.

J. What are you afraid of? Mom?

L. Fear of man.

J. Jesus is here for you. Do you see Jesus here? Do you know Mr. Jesus?

L. Yes.

J. (Speaking for Jesus) You don't have to live in fear. You can come out. Your masters are gone. I'm here for you. These men love you, are for you. They won't hurt you.

Do you see what I have for you?

L. Not sure.

J. My hand. Will you take it?

L. Yes.

J. Will you forgive big Lon?

L. Yes.

J. Big Lon, welcome little Lon back. Forgive him. Be kind to him.

Lon, repeat what I say. "I welcome little Lon back. I embrace little Lon."

Jesus, finish your deep work of healing. We'll be silent for a bit while Jesus completes the healing. (Time of silence)

J. We stand together against any retaliation. We break the power of the spirit of resentment. We bind all these spirits from retaliating against Lon, his wife, us, and our families.

Session 4

J. (He asked general questions about how Lon's day had gone)

Personally, how are you doing? Is your heart OK?

L. (Told about an insight he had about attention)

J. Wanting attention is good. It's what we were made for. It's good for our young and adult selves.

What is going home going to be like for you?

L. I'll probably share it gently and slowly. My friends aren't into this. I don't know; I'll have to wing it.

J. As an older guide, I wouldn't try to bring these ideas to them. As life goes on, people will come to you and you'll know what's up.

Some other heart issues—something with Jean is not mutual. Maybe it's related to your addiction.

L. Well, trust has to be regained. There will be progress and healing. That's where we're going. But how do I speed up the healing?

J. As a woman, what's her deep question?

L. Am I lovely.

J. The lie toward you is your heart is not good. I see your heart Lon. You're a good man. For her, the battle lie is

"See, you weren't enough for him." So that's where you need to rescue her and come strongly with words. "Jean, I wasn't looking for another woman."

L. During our first session together with the therapist, I was emotionless. She stood up and said, "Show me this is important to you!"

J. She would feel "I'm not worth fighting for." Tell her that "the risk was for you. I want my heart back so I can offer it to you."

Healing in the Four Streams is a process. Christ takes us into it, then lets us take a breath. Then back in, etc. We'll continue to work through things as things come up.

Now, what do you need to hear from God? What question?

L. What healing has occurred? Do I need to continue my counseling and SA (like AA, but for sex addicts) meetings?

J. What we did wasn't an instant fix. But it cleared things up so you can walk with God. I'd say stay with the counseling and SA for awhile. What you'll discover is some freedom as you keep doing those things.

I'd counsel you to bring the cross between you and your parents. You'll feel more able to walk the walk you want now.

Allow desire to surface. You don't have to live a small life. "Lon, your heart matters" is what God is saying in all this.

Let's pray and just listen to see what Jesus wants to say. (John prayed) Whatever we hear, we'll share, okay?

J. I hear "this is just the beginning. There's more freedom." Where does that land in your heart?

L. It allows me to walk in grace, but with expectation. There's still a war.

J. There's more. What does your heart do if its "just a beginning?"

L. It will require trust for Christ to help. I can't just take over.

J. Yeah. You don't have to do anything. Jesus has more. Jesus, what else are you saying?

L. I hear "I'm going to take care of you." I don't know what that looks like.

J. Yeah, your analytical self wants to know, but it's not needed. We can just say "okay, I'll take it."

Jesus, what else about the future? "Release your parents to me." I think there's a lot there.

L. I still want to hear my parents say that they love me and think I'm great.

J. Our parents, though good, are wrong about us. Practice releasing your parents to Jesus.

L. After our second session, my roommate Tim said, "What if your parents are wrong about you?"

J. What makes family kryptonite is that they are the last word, the verdict on us. We give them to Jesus.

Jesus, is there anything else for Lon?

There's something from me: I want you to know I love you. I love the impishness of the boy. But I also love what I see in the man.

Christ, our request is for all these words to matter, to sink in. Identify Jean's enemies for Lon. We pray for healing in her heart and beauty and for redemption in their marriage.

(End of the sessions)

As a learner of Four Streams, ask yourself and Jesus what you can learn from reading this transcript. Write your responses below, if you like.

-

-

-

-

I suggest you reflect on what you wrote above before you do Four Streams with someone.

Resources:

- RansomedHeart.com (events, books & audio, podcasts)

- TexasBandOfBrothers.org (events, articles on Resources page)

- kclehman.com (inner-healing articles)

- *The Life Model: Living from the Heart Jesus Gave You* by James G. Friesen, PhD., et al; Shepherd's House, Inc. 2000 (concise, practical, written from both experience and research; includes material on stages of maturity and the importance of community)

- *Soul Talk* by Larry Crabb, Integrity Publishers, 2003 (practical steps in productive listening and talking on a deep level).

- *Hind's Feet on High Places* by Hanna Hurnard, Tyndale House, 1997 (allegory of the disciple's journey with Jesus which illustrates the process of inner healing, spiritual warfare, and counseling, in the context of a disciple).

www.ingramcontent.com/pod-product-compliance
Lightning Source LLC
Chambersburg PA
CBHW071622040426
42452CB00009B/1437